FEARLESS

Contemplative Coloring for All People.

An exploration of original, hand drawn art by Angel Cheney.

Art is a beautiful medium for relaxation, stress relief, therapy, and enjoyment. It is our hope that as you travel through these pages you will be encouraged by what you find and experience. Some of the pages include areas of white space where you can add your own thoughts, dreams, or doodles. Enjoy!

About the artist:
Angel Cheney is an artist, singer/songwriter, poet, and author from the Indianapolis, IN area. She is passionate about taking people on a journey with her through art, words, and music. Check out more of her work at:

www.angelcheney.com

**Stay tuned!
Exciting new books of
Contemplative Coloring
for All People
COMING SOON!**

Speak the TRUTH
you are carrying in your heart
like hidden treasure.

I AM

FULL

OF

LIFE.

I am peacefully allowing my life to unfold.

I

AM

SAFE

I AM
LETTING GO
OF THE PAST,
PRESENT
IN THIS MOMENT,

AND MOVING
FORWARD
WITH
CONFIDENCE.

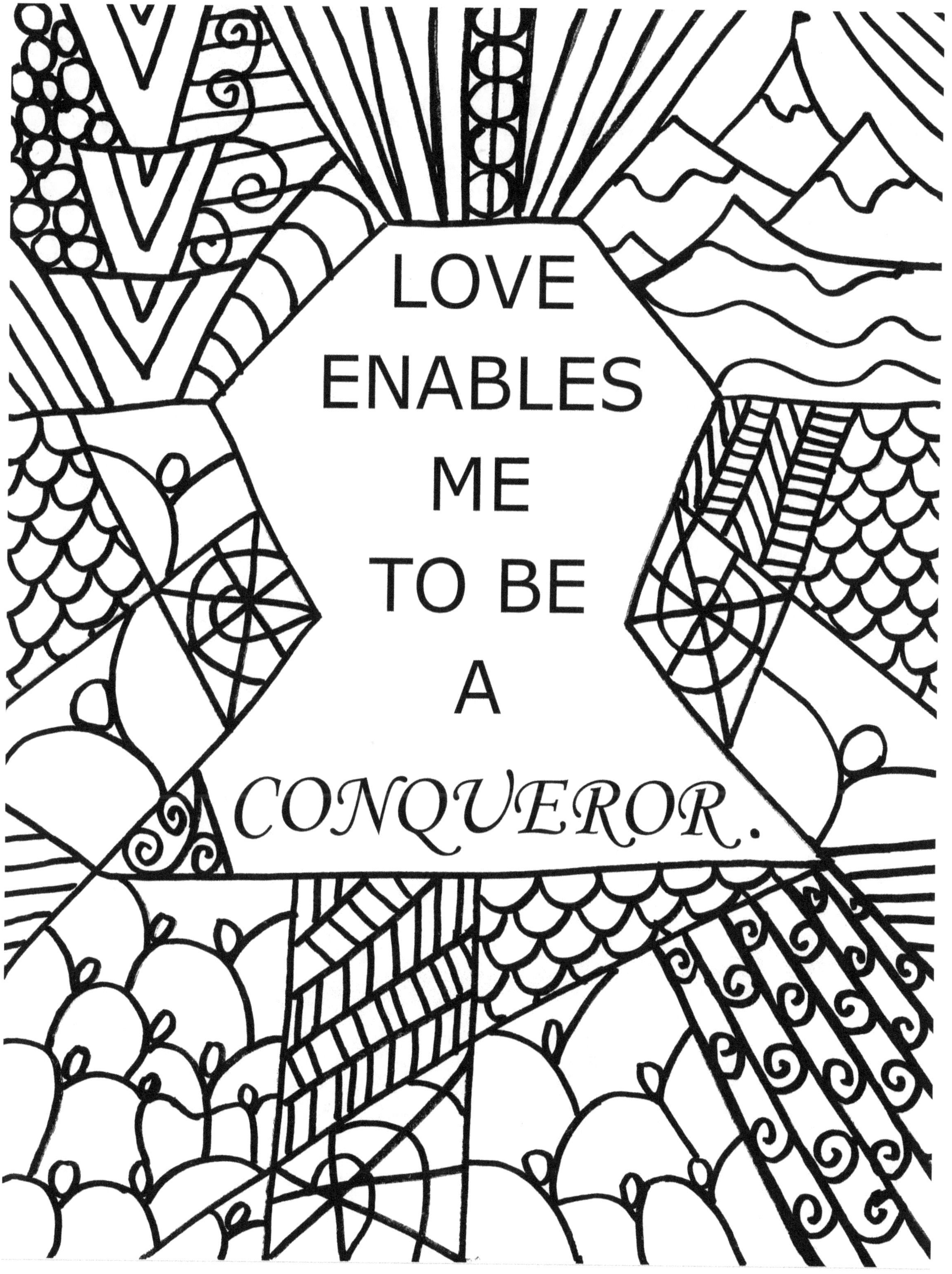
LOVE
ENABLES
ME
TO BE
A
CONQUEROR.

I AM GRATEFUL FOR:

1.

2.

3.

4.

5.

I am Beautiful

I am Loved

I AM ENOUGH

COURAGE

EMBRACE
LOVE,

RELEASE
FEAR.

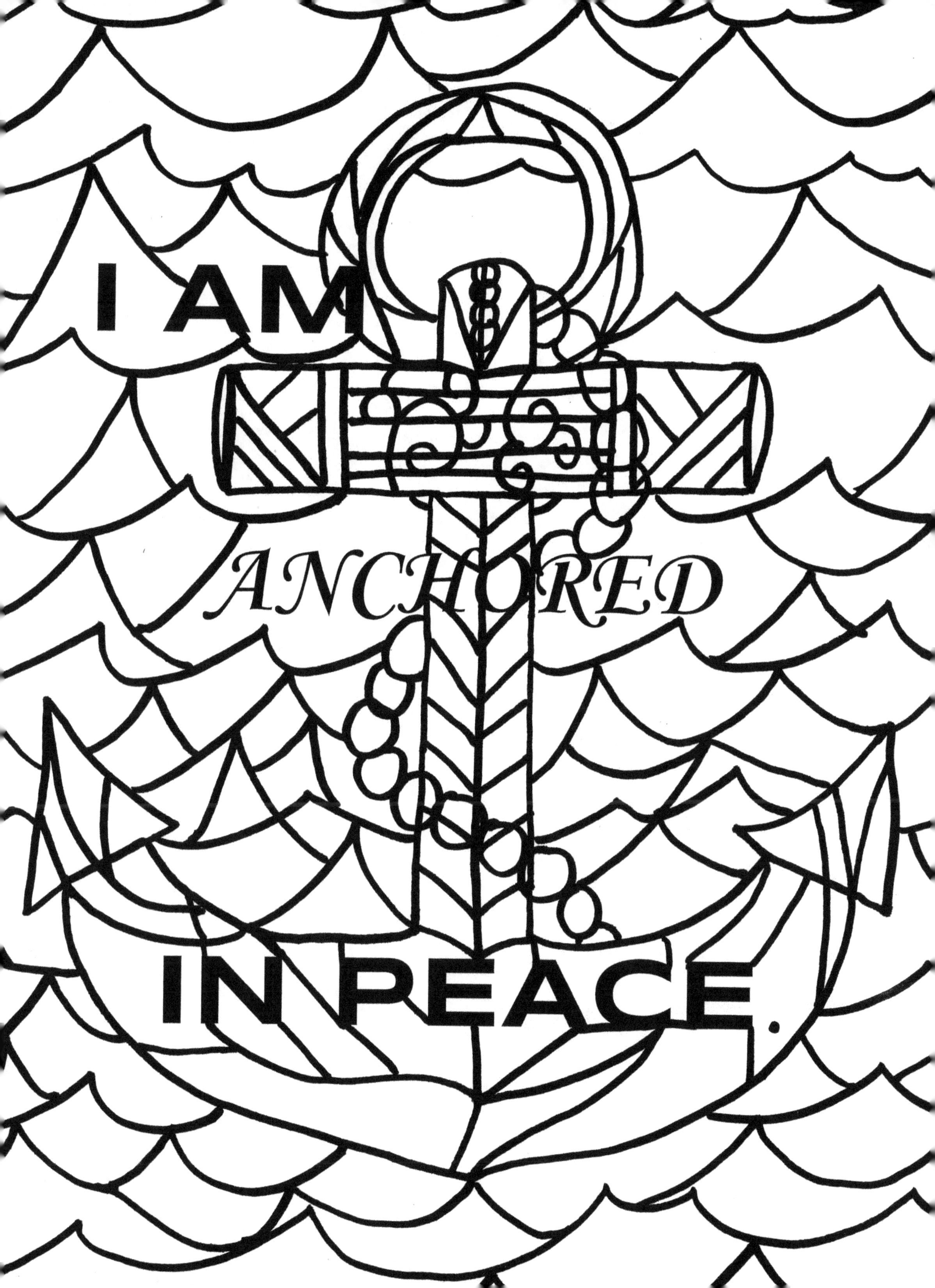
I AM
ANCHORED
IN PEACE.

Rise Above

Plant truth
and reap
a harvest
of
LOVE.

I AM BRAVE.

Design your own coat of arms

I LOVE AND DEEPLY CARE FOR MY MIND, BODY, AND SOUL.